STYLES

HOW TO TELL A
FABLE

Suri Rosen

🌳 Crabtree Publishing Company

www.crabtreebooks.com

Text STYLES

Author: Suri Rosen

Coordinating editor: Reagan Miller

Publishing plan research and development:
Sean Charlebois, Reagan Miller
Crabtree Publishing Company

Editorial director: Kathy Middleton

Print coordinator: Katherine Berti

Production coordinator: Margaret Salter

Prepress technician: Samara Parent

Logo design: Samantha Crabtree

Product development: Victory Productions, Inc.

Content Editor: Janet Stone

Photo research: Tracy Vancelette

Front cover: Characters from the following fables appear: The Goose That Laid the Golden Eggs; The Three Little Pigs, The Tortoise and the Hare, and The Hare and the Elephant King.

Title page: One of Aesop's fables describes a crafty fox who outwits a crow and takes his dinner of delicious grapes.

Photographs:

Adobe Images: title page (grapes)

The Granger Collection, NYC: 25 (bottom)

Object Gear: 15 (right)

Wikimedia Commons: cover (Project Gutenberg archives: The Goose that Laid the Golden Eggs; Jean Granville: The Tortoise and the Hare; Maler von Syrischer: The Hare and the Elephant King, Library of Congress: Three Little Pigs)

Shutterstock: All other images

Illustrations:

Barbara Bedell: front cover (owl), 19 (jackal), 21 (owl)

Katherine Berti: 8 (fox)

Margaret Amy Salter: 8 (Kodiak bear, Arabian horse), 9 (spider monkey)

Cataloguing in Publication data is available at Library and Archives Canada.

Cataloging-in-Publication data is available at Library of Congress.

Crabtree Publishing Company

www.crabtreebooks.com   1-800-387-7650

Printed in Canada/082011/MA20110714

Published in Canada
Crabtree Publishing
616 Welland Ave.
St. Catharines, Ontario
L2M 5V6

Published in the United States
Crabtree Publishing
PMB 59051
350 Fifth Avenue, 59th Floor
New York, New York 10118

Published in the United Kingdom
Crabtree Publishing
Maritime House
Basin Road North, Hove
BN41 1WR

Published in Australia
Crabtree Publishing
3 Charles Street
Coburg North
VIC 3058

Contents

What is a Fable?

"Honesty is the best policy." "If at first you don't succeed, try, try again." Have you heard these sayings before? These well-known sayings can be traced back to stories that were first told thousands of years ago! These stories are called fables. A **fable** is a short, simple story that teaches an important lesson. The lesson is called a **moral**. Morals are statements of how we should behave.

Fables are found in countries all over the world. Fables share some common features:

The common elements of a fable are:

- Fables were passed from generation to generation through word of mouth.

- The characters are often animals who act and talk like humans.

- A fable helps the reader understand human behavior.

- A fable ends with a moral or a lesson.

In this book, you will learn about the characteristics of fables. You will read some fables and even write a fable of your own!

People have been telling fables for thousands of years!

Most of the fables we know today came from a Greek slave known as Aesop. Aesop was born in 620 B.C.E. A great storyteller, he wrote and collected hundreds of fables and told them orally.

Fables teach a lesson, are easy to relate to, and connect us with other cultures. They also involve animals found in the story's culture.

Learn more about the various countries and cultures from which the stories come.

Reflects cultural beliefs

We can learn about different cultures by reading fables. The animal characters that are found in fables tell us about the animals that can be found in those countries. The lessons that fables teach us show something about the cultures they come from.

Fables can have more than one lesson.

Fables use various animals in different ways to portray human strengths and weaknesses in order to pass down wisdom from one generation to the next.

Fables are short stories that have been told for thousands of years. People told fables to teach the listeners and entertain them at the same time. Fables offer lessons about life and ourselves. They show us how we should behave.

Behaving badly will always get a character into trouble in a fable. Fables are tales that show us how being wise and making good choices are always rewarded.

Another important group of fables is called the Panchatantra. These are ancient Indian fables that were collected in the third century B.C.E. These stories were based on very old fables that had been around thousands of years before that!

The Boy Who Cried Wolf

—a retelling of a fable by Aesop

There once was a young shepherd who watched over a flock of sheep just outside his small village. Every morning, the boy led the sheep up a small hill to a pasture and watched over them as they nibbled the grass and drank from a small pond.

The boy spent his days alone with the sheep. He had no one to talk to or play with. Every day he grew more and more bored. The minutes began to feel like hours.

One day, the boy had an idea. He decided to pretend that a wolf had come to hurt the sheep.

The boy stood on the hill and faced the village below. He took a deep breath and yelled as loudly as he could, "Wolf! Wolf! The wolf is chasing the sheep!"

The men from the village ran up the hill as fast as they could to help the boy. They looked around but saw no wolf. "Where is the wolf?" they asked.

The boy burst into laughter. How simple these men were, he thought. "I was just pretending," he said, still laughing. What a wonderful way to break up a boring afternoon!

The men stared at the grinning boy. "That is not funny!" said the men. They turned and stomped back down the hill to the village.

The next day, the boy sat alone on the hill watching the sheep. Once again he grew bored. It had been so exciting when the men came running when he called. He wanted to have a bit more fun.

The boy stood on the hill and faced the village below. He took a deep breath and yelled as loudly as he could, "Wolf! Wolf! The wolf is chasing the sheep!"

The men from the village again raced up the hill to help the boy. "Where is the wolf?" they asked as they scanned the pasture.

The boy burst out laughing again. It was so easy to fool these simple people.

"There is no wolf," answered the boy. "It was just a joke."

"How dare you waste our time," said one man, spitting out the words. "Call us only when there is real trouble!" He turned around and stomped back down the hill to the the village. The other men followed him in angry silence.

The next day the boy lay on the grass and felt the warm sun on his face. The sheep began to bleat loudly. The boy sat up.

In the distance, the boy saw a wolf coming toward the flock of sheep. The boy's heart began to race.

He cried out, "Wolf! There's a wolf in the pasture! Please! Someone come right away. The sheep are scared!"

The wolf inched closer. The sheep suddenly ran off in different directions.

"Wooolf," the boy yelled. "He is getting closer!" The boy ran to the edge of the hill and looked at the village below. He could see the people in the village working and going on with their day. Nobody was listening to his calls for help. Nobody was racing up the hill to help him.

The boy picked up a rock. His hands shook as the wolf came closer. The boy's heart hammered in his chest. He was all alone now. He raised his hand and threw the rock at the wolf. The rock hit the wolf's leg. The wolf growled. It turned and limped back into the forest.

The sheep were now spread out over the hill. The boy spent the rest of the afternoon rounding them up without any help from anyone.

Fable Characters

Characters in fables are different than characters in other kinds of stories. Characters in fables can be people, animals, or other creatures. The characters are very simple. We usually know very little about them. A character in a fable has one important trait. A trait is a part of a character's personality. We learn about characters and their traits by what they do. Read the passages below.

Once again the boy grew bored. It had been so exciting when the men of the village came running out to the pasture. He wanted to have a bit more fun.

The boy burst out laughing again. It was so easy to fool these simple men.

We do not know much about the boy. We do understand something important, though. The boy likes to tell lies as a joke. He laughs at the men for running to help him. He does not care that fooling the men will waste their time.

Certain animals are related to specific traits. For example, a fox is often sly and selfish, a sheep is often shy and fearful, and a lion is often strong yet arrogant or overconfident. Their character trait is what matters in the fable.

We do not know much about the village men who answer the boy's cries for help. They all trust the boy and believe him when he asks for their help. They are hard workers, but they are willing to stop work and come to help him. They act responsibly.

the boy

actions: makes the villagers leave their work
laughs at the villagers

traits: inconsiderate
irresponsible

the villagers

actions: come to help the boy

traits: hard-working
responsible

● **Why do we not need to know more about the boy? Does it matter what he looks like or what his name is? The boy is in a fable so we can learn lessons from the way he acts.**

Traits of a Character

Think of a good character for your own fable. What trait does this character have? You might want to choose an animal. Match a trait with the animal. What animal would be loud and bossy? What animal would be very clever or very lazy? List some characters and their traits.

Dialogue: The Characters Talk

When characters speak, it is called **dialogue**. Quotation marks (" ") are always placed around a character's exact words. Dialogue makes characters seem like real people and helps the story come alive. We can learn about a person by what they say and how they say it.

The man's words are angry, and he spits out his words. This helps you picture him in your mind.

> *"How dare you waste our time," he said, spitting out the words.*

● **Read some of the dialogue in the fable a few times. Stress or emphasize different words. Use your voice to add feelings and emotion.**

Dialogue also moves a story forward. Every time the boy yells wolf, something happens. The men come running in the beginning because they trust the boy. Then they stop believing him when he keeps lying.

● **Sheep Have Their Say**

Imagine that it is the day after the wolf came to the pasture. These are not happy sheep. Imagine that these sheep are able to talk and they have a meeting. They decide that they are going to fire the boy. Give reasons why they are angry. Write dialogue for their meeting.

Talking the Talk

Add some more dialogue for the village men as they leave the pasture. Imagine what they might say to each other on their way back to the village. What would they say to each other about the boy and what is going on? Show their feelings in the dialogue.

Setting: Here, There, or Anywhere

The setting is the *place* where the story happens. It is also the *time* period when the story takes place. But fables are different from other tales. Fables do not really give much detail about the setting. There are just enough details to help us understand the action. They often take place in a forest or a village. These places could be almost anywhere in the world.

Fables take place sometime in the past, because these fables were created many, many years ago. "The Boy Who Cried Wolf" is one of the most famous fables written by Aesop, the ancient Greek storyteller. This fable is still repeated all over the world because it still has a lesson to teach us. The fables have not been changed to include modern things like cars or computers.

● **Does it matter what country or culture this fable comes from? Do we need to know that it comes from ancient Greece? Why or why not?**

A young shepherd watched over a flock of sheep just outside his small village. Every day he followed the sheep up a small mountain and guarded them as they nibbled the grass and drank from a small pond.

We know the boy is a shepherd. We know that the sheep are grazing in a pasture. They are far enough away to make it hard for men to come and help, but they are not so far away that they cannot hear the boy.

● **Draw the Setting**
Look back at your list of characters for a fable. Draw a setting for one of them. Include just a few details. For example, if you draw a house, make it simple. Hold on to this drawing for when you write your own fable.

Fable Plots: Simple Plot, Big Lesson

The **plot** is what happens in a story. A fable has a very simple plot. The plot always starts with a single problem. The main character has a problem and must find a way to solve it. Sometimes the character wants something and must figure out how to get it. The problem is also called **conflict**. The events are all about how the problem gets solved.

The turning point, or **climax**, is the moment of greatest excitement. In a fable, it is often the moment when the main character realizes something. It usually comes close to the end of the fable. The ending wraps up the story. The ending is called the **resolution**.

⬤ **Why do you think the villagers are not coming to help the boy? Does the boy understand that his lies caused this to happen? Why is this moment so important in the story?**

A Problem for a Fable

Choose a character for a fable. What does the character want? How can the character get it? Explain how your character will solve the problem. Be creative. With fable animals, almost anything goes! Save this idea to use in your own fable.

Story Map for "The Boy Who Cried Wolf"

Characters	boy, villagers
Setting	a pasture, a long time ago
Problem	The boy is bored.
Events	1. The bored boy watches sheep.
	2. The boy pretends there is a wolf and calls for help.
	3. The men come to save the sheep.
	4. The boy cries wolf again and the men return.
	5. Climax: The boy calls out for help but the men do not come this time.
Resolution	The boy must fight the wolf and gather the sheep on his own.
Lesson	The boy learns that nobody believes a liar, even when he tells the truth.

Like "The Boy Who Cried Wolf," the plots of fables often include **repetition**. The same act is repeated two or three times. The repetition builds suspense.

Some fables are funny. The use of repeated words and actions builds the humor as well as the suspense. In the fable "The Three Little Pigs," each of the three little pigs builds a house. One builds his house out of straw. One builds his house out of sticks. The third builds his house out of bricks. The action and dialogue are repeated three times. But the third time, the result is different. Here's an example of repetition from the fable "The Three Little Pigs."

The wolf came to the house made of straw. "Let me in, let me in," said the wolf. "Or I'll huff and I'll puff and I'll blow your house in!"

"Not by the hair of my chinny chin chin!" cried the little pig.

So the wolf huffed and he puffed and he blew the house in.

Make a Prediction
Read the fable "The Little Red Hen." After she asks her friends to help her a second time, predict what will happen next. Write down what you think the lesson is. Then keep reading to see if the ending matches your prediction and the lesson you think the fable teaches.

 What did you think when the boy cried wolf the second time? Were you worried about what might happen next? Did the way the villagers responded the third time surprise you?

The wolf came to the house made of sticks. "Let me in, let me in," said the wolf. "Or I'll huff and I'll puff and I'll blow your house in!"

"Not by the hair of my chinny chin chin!" cried the little pig.

So the wolf huffed and he puffed and he blew the house in.

Repetition helps us predict the ending. How do you think the fable of the three little pigs ends?

Theme: The Moral of the Fable

The plot is what the fable is about. A **theme** is the message of the fable. Fables always end with an important life lesson. This lesson is also called a moral. The whole purpose of the fable is to teach this lesson. Sometimes, the moral is stated at the end of the fable. Sometimes we have to think about the fable and find the lesson ourselves.

A fable entertains us with a good story. The moral gives us words to live by. The moral is an idea that is expressed very clearly through the actions and events. We see what the lesson means.

Moral: Nobody believes a liar, even when he tells the truth.

- What does this moral teach us?
- What might happen if we tell lies?
- How should we behave?

The Theme Queen

The Theme Queen is a talk-show host. She would like to interview you about this fable. She seems very surprised by the boy in the fable. Explain to her what the boy did. Tell what important lesson the boy learned, and explain the moral of the story.

Creative Response to the Fable

Funny Fables!

Turn the fable "The Boy who Cried Wolf" into a comic book. Draw a picture of the setting in your first box, and add a title. In each box after that, include pictures of the main events. In your last box draw the resolution. Make sure that the boxes are in order of the story!

A News Report: Coming to you live from the pasture!

Pretend that you are a reporter. You are telling TV viewers about the events in this fable. Imagine that you are at the pasture. Perform a live report. Interview some of the people or animals in the story. Ask them to tell their thoughts about the events.

Puppet Show

Make hand puppets out of socks for the wolf and the boy. Retell the fable from the wolf's point of view. What did the wolf think about the boy? What did he think every time the boy yelled out "wolf"?

Fables from India

"The Boy Who Cried Wolf" was written by a Greek writer named Aesop. Aesop lived over 2,500 years ago. He wrote over 600 fables that are still read today. These fables are known all over the world.

Another group of fables are from India. These fables belong to the Panchatantra. These stories are almost as old as Aesop's fables and were written in 300 B.C.E. The Panchatantra fables are also filled with animals, creatures, and spirits. All of them talk and behave like people.

The Panchatantra fable "The Blue Jackal" is a lot like "The Boy Who Cried Wolf." The main character—the jackal—is very clever. Like the boy who cried wolf, the jackal fools the other characters. Both fables start with a main character that has a problem. Their problems cause some interesting events. At the end of the fable, the moral becomes clear. As in every fable, the main character always gets what he deserves!

The Blue Jackal

There once was a *jackal* named Fierce-Howl. He lived alone in a cave at the edge of a town. He was always hungry and was forever looking for food. One night his empty stomach hurt so much that he had to do something. He wandered into the town. It was not a safe place for a jackal. He searched for some food around town. He found a heap of garbage and began sniffing and scratching it. He hoped he would find something to eat.

A pack of dogs heard his sounds and surrounded him. They nipped at his feet with their sharp teeth. The dogs growled and barked. Terrified, Fierce-Howl turned away from the pack. He fled from the garbage heap, and raced through the town. The dogs chased him, barking and biting him along the way.

Fierce-Howl did not know where to go. He bolted through the streets with the dogs on his heels. His heart pounded with fear. He looked for hiding places but could not find any.

The jackal suddenly spotted an open door to a house. Finally, he thought, I am safe! He jumped through the doorway and landed in a big pot of blue dye! He climbed out of the pot. His fur was completely blue. Somehow, he escaped from the town and returned to the forest.

When he arrived in the forest, the other animals spotted him right away. What was this strange blue creature? No one had ever seen anything like it. They fled in terror away from Fierce-Howl. Fierce-Howl saw their fear.

"Why do you run away?" he called out to them.

But then Fierce-Howl had an idea. "I am king of all of the creatures of the forest," he said to them.

The lions, tigers, leopards, monkeys, and rabbits bowed before him. "How may we serve you?" they asked.

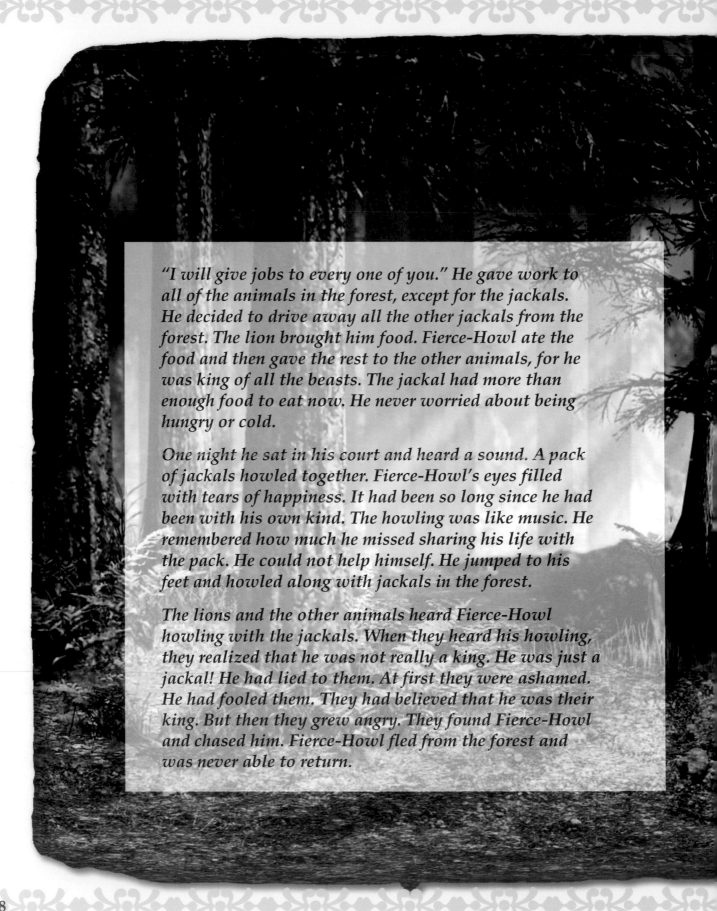

"I will give jobs to every one of you." He gave work to all of the animals in the forest, except for the jackals. He decided to drive away all the other jackals from the forest. The lion brought him food. Fierce-Howl ate the food and then gave the rest to the other animals, for he was king of all the beasts. The jackal had more than enough food to eat now. He never worried about being hungry or cold.

One night he sat in his court and heard a sound. A pack of jackals howled together. Fierce-Howl's eyes filled with tears of happiness. It had been so long since he had been with his own kind. The howling was like music. He remembered how much he missed sharing his life with the pack. He could not help himself. He jumped to his feet and howled along with jackals in the forest.

The lions and the other animals heard Fierce-Howl howling with the jackals. When they heard his howling, they realized that he was not really a king. He was just a jackal! He had lied to them. At first they were ashamed. He had fooled them. They had believed that he was their king. But then they grew angry. They found Fierce-Howl and chased him. Fierce-Howl fled from the forest and was never able to return.

What a Character!

The main character in this fable is Fierce-Howl, the jackal. Even though he is an animal, he talks and acts like a person. And because this is a fable, we know very little about him.

We see a bit about what he is like by the way he acts as the story moves forward. At the start of the fable, he is hungry. As the story continues we see other parts of his character. He is scared when the dogs chase him. When he enters the forest, he thinks of a good lie. He is clever. Finally, when he hears the other jackals howling, we see that he is lonely.

But then Fierce-Howl had an idea. "I am king of all of the creatures of the forest," he said to them.

He gave work to all of the animals in the forest, except for the jackals. He decided to drive away all the jackals from the forest. Fierce-Howl ate the food and then gave the rest to the other animals, for he was king of all the beasts.

What character traits does the jackal show when he gets his idea to become a king? Did you feel sorry for the jackal at the beginning of the fable? Do your feelings about him change when you read this part?

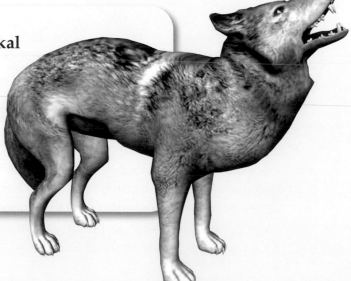

 At the end of the fable, the jackal has been chased from his home in the forest. He is once again just a jackal, not a strange animal that is a king. But we hope that he has learned an important lesson! Do you think the jackal is wise at the end?

● **Compare and contrast the jackal and the boy who cried wolf. How do you think they are different? How are they alike? Do they act the same? Do they want the same things?**

Jackal — hungry, likes to feel special

— lonely, clever

Boy — bored, wants to have some fun

A Picture Is Worth Many Words

There are all kinds of characters in fables. Some are wise and some are foolish. Some are honest and some do not tell the truth. Look back at the characters you are developing for a fable. Choose one. Focus on the character's trait. How would a timid rabbit look? Would a lazy lion be sitting up or lying down? Make your character come alive!

Dialogue: Formal Language

 Dialogue helps bring the characters to life. In the first part of the fable, the jackal spends his time hiding and being chased. In the second part, he makes himself king of the forest. All the animals serve him.

 What does this dialogue show us about the jackal? Why does he tell the animals that he is their king?

The lions, tigers, leopards, monkeys, and rabbits bowed before him. "How may we serve you?" they asked.

"I will give jobs to every one of you."

The dialogue also moves the story along. We see from that dialogue that the jackal decides to act like a powerful animal. The animals in the forest accept that he is their king.

The dialogue in this fable is formal. The characters do not speak the way people speak in conversations. Imagine if those lines were written like this instead:

All the animals nodded to the jackal. "Hey, what do you want us to do?" they asked.

"I am in charge of you," he said. "And I am going to give all of you stuff to do."

Write More Dialogue
Add dialogue to the fable. Imagine that a rabbit suspects that he's just a jackal. The rabbit talks to the jackal, before the other animals find out the truth. Write dialogue for them. Think of how you are going to show characters' thoughts and feelings through the words they use.

Can you hear the difference? The formal language makes the fable more important. People use formal language on important occasions. They want us to remember their words. Storytellers told fables to help us learn. We pay more attention to the lesson because of the language.

Setting: Where in the World?

"The Blue jackal" is a fable from India. But the setting in this fable could be taking place in any country at almost any time in the past. There are few details about where the story is set. That is the usual way for fables. We do know that the jackal lives in a cave in the forest. We also know the forest is close to a town.

The house in the town is very important to the fable. This is where the jackal jumps into blue dye. The forest is important too. This is where the jackal lives among the other animals. But that is all we really need to know about where the story takes place.

The jackal suddenly spotted an open door to a house. Finally, he thought, I am safe! He jumped through the doorway and landed in a big pot of blue dye! He climbed out of the vat of dye. His fur was completely blue. Somehow, he escaped from the town and returned to the forest.

● Do we really need to know when the story takes place? Fables are timeless. The lessons can be applied to any time, place, and situation.

● Is the setting in this fable like the one in "The Boy Who Cried Wolf"? How are they different?

Describe the Setting
Write some descriptive details for the setting of this fable. Use words that appeal to the senses. What did the dye smell like or feel like? How did the jackal's fur feel after it was covered in dye? What season was it in the forest? What sounds did the animals hear and make?

Plot: The Map of the Fable

The plot is what happens in the story. The jackal's problem—hunger—drives the action. Each event leads to another event. The jackal thinks he's solved the problem, but his dishonesty leads to his punishment.

The turning point, or climax, comes when the jackal hears the other jackals and starts to howl. The other animals suddenly realize that their king is really just a blue jackal. The resolution comes quickly.

A **story map** shows the basic parts of a plot.

Characters: the jackal and other forest animals
Setting: a forest and a town
Problem: The jackal is hungry.
Events:

1. The jackal goes to town to search for food.

2. A pack of dogs chase him.

3. While trying to escape the dogs, the jackal enters a house and falls into a pot of blue dye.

4. The jackal tells the other animals that he is king of all creatures.

5. Climax: The jackal howls and the other animals discover he is a jackal, not a king.

Resolution: The animals chase the jackal out of the forest. He is not allowed to return to the forest.

Lesson: It is always better to be yourself instead of pretending to be someone else.

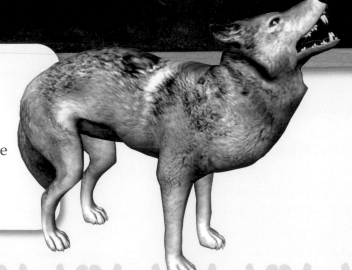

Map Your Fable

Complete a story map for your favorite fable or for a fable that you would like to write. Be sure to include the climax. Write the lesson of the fable in the box for the resolution.

Theme: The Lesson We Learn

 Themes are lessons, or morals, that we learn from fables.

The jackal in this fable goes from hunger and danger to becoming king of the forest. But the fable does not end on this happy note.

These events contain the lesson of this fable. The moral here is that it doesn't pay to pretend to be someone you're not. The jackal cannot escape who he really is. Now he must leave his home.

⬤ **What would happen if you tried to act like someone you were not?**

The lions and the other animals heard Fierce-Howl howling with the jackals. When they heard his howling, they realized that he was not really a king. He was just a jackal! He had lied to them. At first they were ashamed. He had fooled them. They had believed that he was their king. But then they grew angry. They found Fierce-Howl and chased him. Fierce-Howl fled from the forest and was never able to return.

Read the fable "The Dog and His Shadow." This very short fable teaches us an important lesson. Put yourself in the dog's place as you read.

The Dog and His Shadow

A dog was crossing a stream with a piece of meat in his mouth. He looked down in the water and saw a dog carrying a piece of meat twice the size. He did not realize that it was his own reflection. He wanted the bigger piece of meat! He barked at the dog and the meat fell out of his mouth. In the end the dog was left with nothing.

The moral of this fable is, "Be happy with what you have."

⬤ **How did you feel at the end? How can you use this lesson in your own life?**

⬤ **Write a Letter**
Write a letter to the jackal. Tell the jackal what mistakes he made and how he should live his life now.

Creative Response to the Fable

Make a Mask

Make a mask of the jackal. Draw a picture of a jackal on cardboard. Use blue markers, pencil crayons, or paint to color him. Make holes for the eyes. Cut out the drawing and glue it to a craft stick. Use your mask to retell the fable.

Make a Board Game

Choose a fable that you like and list all the events. Then draw a game board on poster board. Draw one square for each event. If you like, you can add a drawing to each square. Add a few squares in between each event to make the game board longer. Your game board should have at least twenty squares. Label one end **Start** and one end **Moral**. Cut out a small picture of a jackal, a lion, or any other animal to use as markers. Roll the dice. If you land on an even number, you move ahead. If you land on an odd number you have to go back to Start. The first player to reach the end of the game yells, "I got plot!" and wins.

An En-Chant-ing Chant!

In this fable, the main character drives away the other jackals when he becomes king of the forest. The jackals are very unhappy and decide to write a chant. Write a chant that the jackals could shout together when they demand to be allowed back in the forest.

Writing a Fable

The time has come to write your own fable. By now you have ideas for character, dialogue, setting, and plot. Let's start writing a fable!

1 Prewriting

Because the purpose of a fable is to teach a lesson, start with the lesson you want to teach with your fable. Think of something that is important for people to know. Here is a list to get you started:

- **Don't put off until tomorrow what you can do today.**
- **Look before you leap.**
- **Do what you know how to do best.**
- **Be careful what you say about others.**

2 Explore a Character

Choose a character that will be at the center of your fable. Give your character one strong trait. Your character may be foolish or wise, carefree or serious. Will this trait get the character into trouble?

3 Explore the Problem

Now put your character together with a problem. Write a sentence that tells about the character and the problem.

- **A carefree grasshopper plays all day instead of working.**
- **A foolish monkey tries to be as strong as an elephant.**
- **A selfish girl doesn't want to share.**
- **A lazy donkey decides to cheat instead of study hard.**

4 The Main Events

Use a story map to begin to plan the events in your story. Keep the lesson in mind as you write your events. Include only key events in your fable. Remember, fables are short!

Write a First Draft

Put all your ideas down on paper. Don't worry about getting everything right. This is just a first draft to get you started. Use a pencil and write lightly so that you can erase your mistakes when you revise.

Fable Checklist:

- Do I have a character with a strong trait?
- Does the character want something?
- Do the events focus on the problem?
- Does my fable end with a moral?

Abdul chose a lesson that he wanted people to learn. His main character is a foolish monkey who wants to keep the fox from stealing his food. He thinks he can solve the problem by becoming as big as an elephant. Here is his first draft. It has some mistakes in it.

- Read your fable to two friends. Watch their faces as you read. Were there parts of the fable that made them smile or look sad?

- Ask them if they understood the story. Does the story make sense to them? Is it interesting? Could they get a good picture in their mind?

Once there was a monkey and a fox. The fox always stole his food. The monkey wished that he could be as big as an elephant. That way he would be so strong that the fox would never dare take his food.

So the monkey started eating elephant food. He ate cabbage, lettuce, and grass. He ate all day long so he could have as much as an elephant would eat. But his stomach hurt him so much he couldn't do anything. His stomach hurt and he couldn't climb any more. The fox found him lying on the ground weak and in pain.

"Foolish animal," said the fox to the monkey". Not only can you never become a different animal, you can't even be your own animal any more".

6 Revise Your Fable

Reread your fable. Now is your chance to change it and make it even better.

● **Does the plot make sense?**

● **Would adding another event make the fable clearer?**

● **Does it have a lesson or moral?**

Abdul revised his first draft. He made his beginning stronger. He made changes to show how foolish the monkey was.

A monkey was mad because the fox always stole his seeds, nuts, and bananas. One day he complained about this to the elephant.

"Elephant," said the monkey; "I wish I could be huge and strong like you. What do you eat?"

"I eat cabbage, lettuce, and bananas," the elephant answered." Hundreds of pounds every day."

The monkey decided to eat hundreds of pounds of elephant food all day. Then he would be as big and strong as an elephant. He ate all day. He grew big but he did not grow strong. He just grew big and round. One morning, the monkey was so big he couldn't even roll over.

The fox found the monkey lying on the ground in pain. The monkey hurt so much that he could not even move.

"Foolish monkey!" said the fox." You can never become a different animal!"

7 Proofread Your Draft

Check carefully for any spelling mistakes or poor grammar. Use the proofreading checklist below to help you.

- Did I indent all paragraphs?
- Did I use capital letters for proper nouns?
- Did I spell each word correctly?
- Did I punctuate dialogue correctly?

Punctuation for Dialogue

- Use quotation marks (" ") around a character's exact words.
- Use a comma to set off a person's exact words.

"I eat lettuce," said the elephant.

- Begin the first word of a quotation with a capital letter and put an end mark before the last quotation mark.
- The monkey asked, "What do you eat, elephant?"

8 Make a Final Copy

Neatly copy your fable onto clean paper. Add a title for your fable. If you'd like, you can write it in colored markers. You can also draw some pictures to show what is happening in your fable.

Think of some other ways to share your fable.

Congratulations! Just like our friend Aesop, you've written a fable!

Glossary

character	The person, animal, or creature in the story
climax	The moment of greatest excitement
conflict	A problem that the main character has to solve; a problem that causes trouble
dialogue	The words that a character speaks
fable	A short story from a long time ago that always teaches a lesson
jackal	A small animal that is related to wolves, dogs, and coyotes
moral	A life lesson taught in a fable
plot	The events that happen in the story
repetition	The repeating of actions or words for emphasis
resolution	The end of the story, when the plot's main problem is solved
setting	The place and the time that the story takes place
shepherd	Someone who watches over sheep all day
story map	A diagram that shows the basic parts of the plot
theme	The message of the story

Index

Further Resources

Books:

Aesop's Fables by Russell Ash. Chronicle Books (1990)

Aesop's Fables by Fiona Waters (editor). Anderson Press (2010)

Chinese Fables And Folktales by Zheng Ma. Tuttle Publishing Company (2010)

The Wise Fool: Fables from the Islamic World by Husain Shahrukh and Shahrukh Husain. Barefoot Books (2011)

World Myths and Folktales by Carolyn Logan (editor). Holt McDougal (2002)

Websites:

This site includes more than 650 fables!
www.aesopfables.com/

Children can write and publish their own fables on this website.
www.kidsfables.com

This site presents many fables in script form so readers can act out the fables as they read.
www.kidsinco.com/fable

[5]